Looking at . . . Megalosaurus

A Dinosaur from the JURASSIC Period

Weekly Reader®
BOOKS

Published by arrangement with Gareth Stevens, Inc.
Newfield Publications is a federally registered trademark
of Newfield Publications, Inc. Weekly Reader is a federally
registered trademark of Weekly Reader Corporation.

Library of Congress Cataloging-in-Publication Data

Coleman, Graham, 1963-
    Looking at— Megalosaurus / written by Graham Coleman ; illustrated by Tony
Gibbons. — North American ed.
        p. cm. — (The New dinosaur collection.)
    Includes index.
    ISBN 0-8368-1275-1
    1. Megalosaurus—Juvenile literature. [1. Megalosaurus. 2. Dinosaurs.]
I. Gibbons, Tony, ill. II. Title. III. Title: Megalosaurus. IV. Series.
QE862.S3C65 1995
567.9'7—dc20   94-36821

This North American edition first published in 1995 by
Gareth Stevens Publishing
1555 North RiverCenter Drive, Suite 201
Milwaukee, Wisconsin 53212 USA

This U.S. edition © 1995 by Gareth Stevens, Inc. Created with original © 1994
by Quartz Editorial Services, Premier House, 112 Station Road, Edgware HA8
7AQ U.K.

Consultant: Dr. David Norman, Director of the Sedgwick Museum of Geology,
University of Cambridge, England.

Additional artwork by Clare Herronneau.

Printed in the United States of America

Weekly Reader Books Presents

Looking at . . . Megalosaurus

A Dinosaur from the JURASSIC Period

by Graham Coleman

Illustrated by Tony Gibbons

THE NEW
DINOSAUR
COLLECTION

Gareth Stevens Publishing
MILWAUKEE

Contents

Introducing
Megalosaurus

Megalosaurus
(MEG-A-LOW-SAW-RUS)
has a name that means
"giant reptile." That's
hardly surprising. When
it was discovered, it was
one of the largest

Remains of
Megalosaurus
have been found
in many different
parts of the world.
But what did this
creature *really* look like?
Could it run fast? How did it
spend its day? How fierce was it?
Did it have any close relatives?

reptiles the world
had ever known.

Crystal Palace Park
in London, England, is home
to a huge concrete model of
Megalosaurus. It was built in
the nineteenth century by sculptor
Benjamin Waterhouse Hawkins,
but it is not accurate and looks
more like a bear than a dinosaur.

Join us on a
Megalosaurus trek as we set
out to find out all about this
amazing dinosaur.

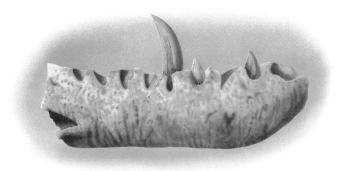

Massive meat-eater

Megalosaurus lived about 155 million years ago during Late Jurassic times. Some scientists think it may have survived longer — well into Early Cretaceous times — but we cannot be sure about this.

This huge creature grew to 30 feet (9 meters) in length and stood more than twice the height of today's average man.

Just imagine how massive it would have been compared to you!

When scientists first assembled the remains of **Megalosaurus**, they made it stand on all four legs, like a bear. It was not until several decades later that they realized **Megalosaurus** actually walked on its two back legs only.

Judging from the footprints of **Megalosaurus** that have been found, this dinosaur walked around at a slow pace much of the time.

It probably traveled no faster than 3.75 to 5 miles (6 to 8 kilometers) per hour, about as fast as an adult human's walking pace. There were few dinosaurs **Megalosaurus** would have needed to run away from, so it did not require speed for survival.

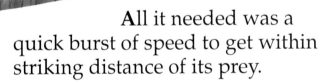

All it needed was a quick burst of speed to get within striking distance of its prey.

Megalosaurus had a large head with incredibly powerful jaws and plenty of strong, sharp teeth. The neck was flexible and strong, too, which meant it was easy for **Megalosaurus** to grab a victim and throw it from side to side. A smaller dinosaur stood little chance of surviving such an attack.

Megaskeleton

the United States, China, India, Africa, Australia, and Greenland.

No single complete skeleton of **Megalosaurus** has yet been found, but this drawing gives a very good idea of what one was like. Paleontologists — experts who study the fossilized remains of prehistoric plants and animals — have now discovered quite a bit about this ferocious carnivore.

Megalosaurus bones have been found in many parts of Europe. Similar types of bones have been found in places as far apart as

The skeleton shown here has been built by piecing together actual bones and imagining what others must have been like.

Megalosaurus had a big skull, as you can see. Its sharp teeth were ideally suited for tearing the flesh of other, smaller dinosaurs.

Just a few snaps of its powerful jaws and any victim would have been a quick meal. The Jurassic world had to be on the lookout for monsters like these.

Megalosaurus could move its short, thick neck easily, which also helped when attacking prey.

Its body was balanced by a long, thick tail. Megalosaurus would have held this tail

forward, and there was one extra, much smaller one, turned back.

But not everything about Megalosaurus was mega. Its two forelimbs were short, although they ended in three frightening, clawed fingers.

Wonderful tracks of this magnificent meat-eater have been found on the Isle of Wight, off the southern coast of Great Britain. From these, and also from the length of their back legs, scientists have been able to guess the weight and speed of Megalosaurus.

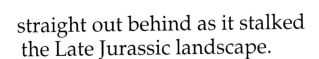

straight out behind as it stalked the Late Jurassic landscape.

Megalosaurus's legs were long and sturdy, too, supporting its body weight of one ton. Three toes on each foot pointed

The first dinosaur to actually be identified from its remains, Megalosaurus had the build of a hunter, as this reconstruction of its skeleton shows.

Giant bone

What could it be? More than three hundred years ago, in the seventeenth century, a museum curator in Oxford, England, named Robert Plot puzzled over an extraordinary fossil that had been found in a nearby quarry.

The fossil was huge, measuring about 24 inches (60 centimeters) in circumference and weighing about 20 pounds (9 kilograms).

Plot examined it carefully and tried to figure out what sort of creature it might have belonged to. At first, he thought it might have been an elephant bone.

Could this elephant have been brought to England hundreds of years previously by the Romans? However, there was no evidence that the Romans had ever brought elephants to England.

If that was not the case, Plot decided, it had to be from a member of an extinct race of giant humans!

Now, of course, we know Plot was mistaken.

The wonderful dinosaur fossil, illustrated here, was in fact from the thighbone of a **Megalosaurus**!

Unfortunately, the fossil has now been lost, but original drawings of it, made long ago, still exist.

Buckland's discovery

Just look at this piece of a huge jawbone fossil! Now picture something nearly three times as long. That's the actual size of this creature's entire jaw. What a monster it must have been!

The fossil shown here is on display at Oxford Museum, England, and it is from a **Megalosaurus**.

This prehistoric beast was described and named by the brilliant scientist and clergyman William Buckland in 1824. At that time, no one knew that the world had once been ruled by such giant creatures. And the word *dinosaur* was not even coined until 1842 by the fossil hunter Richard Owen.

Buckland was something of an eccentric. He claimed to have eaten all sorts of things — including flies called bluebottles!

He also kept a bear as a pet and stored lots of fossil bones and rocks in his house.

Having studied this jaw, a thighbone, ribs, and other bones, Buckland believed they must have come from a creature about 40 feet (12 m) long and 6.5 feet (2 m) tall. How right was he?

Buckland was the first professor of Geology at Oxford University in England.

He would surely be amazed at all the dinosaurs that have been discovered by paleontologists since his day.

Megalosaurus on the prowl

Thump, thump! **Megalosaurus** stomped through the Jurassic forest in a bad mood. It had not eaten for many hours, and it was very hungry.

The young **Camptosaurus** had stopped for a drink by the side of a river. Its family was on the move, searching for some fresh feeding grounds.

There were plenty of ferns around, but they did not interest **Megalosaurus** — it wanted meat!

Suddenly, it spotted something up ahead — a plant-eating dinosaur, **Camptosaurus** (CAMP-TOE-SAW-RUS).

Megalosaurus was soon within striking distance, and it roared loudly. With luck, the appetizing **Camptosaurus** would be much too frightened to run away, and the carnivore would have a good meal.

14

Camptosaurus turned just in time to see the big meat-eater lunge at its neck. The herbivore shrieked as it was knocked off balance. Megalosaurus noticed its victim had a spike on its thumb that could be used as a weapon. But it did not seem that Camptosaurus was going to put up much of a fight.

Just then, however, two much larger Camptosaurus burst onto the scene. They had heard the young one's shrieks and had come to help.

But these two Camptosaurus knew instinctively that Megalosaurus would not want to fight both of them. And they were right.

Megalosaurus leapt at the nearest one. The meat-eater managed to bite into the adult Camptosaurus's neck but let go when the deadly thumb spike pierced its side again and again.

Howling in pain, Megalosaurus trudged away. It was wounded but would live to fight another day.

Megalosaurus was furious at this interruption and snarled at its two new enemies.

For the moment, though, it would go hungry until it felt strong enough to attack once more.

It's not true!

It's odd how many strange ideas people still have about dinosaurs. Filmmakers, for example, have often shown humans battling against dinosaurs. But, of course, dinosaurs became extinct over sixty million years before humans first appeared on Earth. So there is no way any human has ever seen a real, live dinosaur.

Not all dinosaurs were such giant creatures, either. Some, such as tiny **Compsognathus** (<u>KOMP</u>-SOG-<u>NAY</u>-THUS), were only the size of a chicken, as you can see in the illustrations below.

And not all dinosaurs were fierce monsters with sharp teeth and vicious claws. In fact, most dinosaurs were peaceful plant-eaters, like **Diplodocus** (DIP-<u>LOD</u>-OH-KUS), shown at right, that would have fought back only when attacked.

Not all dinosaurs were slow-moving and dim-witted, either. Some, like **Stegosaurus** (<u>STEG</u>-OH-<u>SAW</u>-RUS), opposite top, *did* have a very small brain that was the actual size of the drawing by its side.

But others, such as **Troodon** (<u>TROE</u>-O-DON), below right, had a very large brain for its small size and was more intelligent. It could also run very fast.

Troodon was lightly built, but scientists believe it had sharp eyesight as well as large, slashing claws to defend itself against larger predators.

So if anyone tries to tell you that *all* dinosaurs were fierce creatures, that they fought

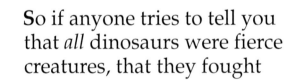

against humans, or that they were stupid, be sure to answer, *"It's not true!"*

A bloody battle

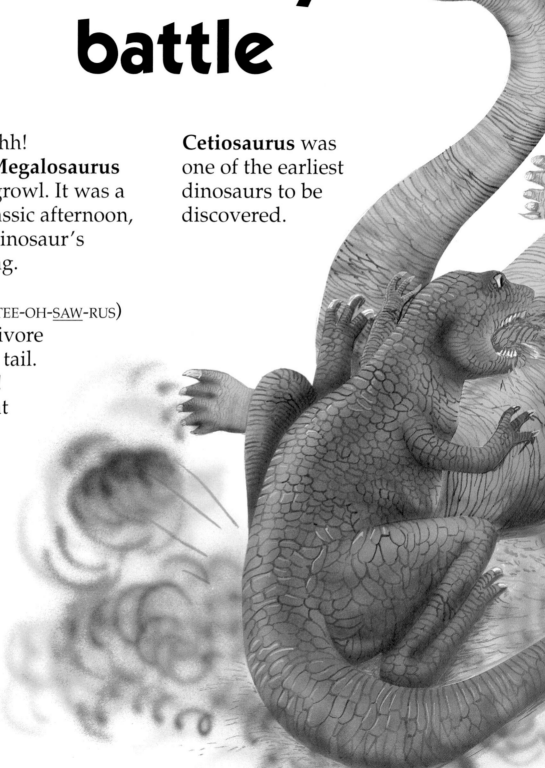

Grrrrhhh! Grrrrhhh!
Time and again **Megalosaurus**
let out a mighty growl. It was a
steaming hot Jurassic afternoon,
and the hungry dinosaur's
temper was flaring.

Cetiosaurus (SEE-TEE-OH-SAW-RUS)
struck at the carnivore
with its whiplash tail.
Thwack! Thwack!
In spite of its great
height, it was
terrified of the
Megalosaurus
and somehow
sensed it might
end up as the
meat-eater's
dinner.

Cetiosaurus was
one of the earliest
dinosaurs to be
discovered.

First unearthed in England in the last century, **Cetiosaurus** was an early sort of **Sauropod** (long-necked, plant-eating dinosaurs). It also had an unusually solid, heavy backbone.

No wonder it was able to strike **Megalosaurus** such a mighty blow.

Megalosaurus snarled ferociously, leapt up, and took a huge bite out of **Cetiosaurus**'s side.

It was a terrible sight. There was blood everywhere. Violence was certainly common in the prehistoric world. The poor herbivore bellowed in pain and keeled over. Before the day was out, it would be no more than a skeleton.

Megalosaurus data

It would have been easy to spot a **Megalosaurus** — if, that is, human beings had existed at the time. These were its main features.

Big head

A mighty hunter, always on the lookout for its next meal of raw dinosaur flesh, **Megalosaurus** had a large head, terrible jaws, and sharp-edged teeth to help it slice great chunks of meat from an unfortunate victim. It must have looked terrifying as it roared!

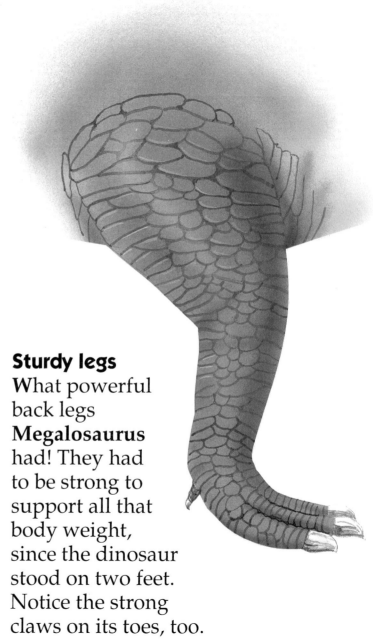

Sturdy legs

What powerful back legs **Megalosaurus** had! They had to be strong to support all that body weight, since the dinosaur stood on two feet. Notice the strong claws on its toes, too.

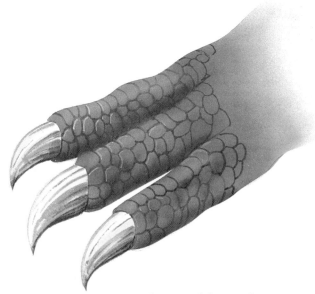

It is easy to imagine this dinosaur moving its head from side to side, viciously shaking a victim in its jaws.

Thick tail

At the other end of **Megalosaurus**'s body was a thick, long tail it probably held out

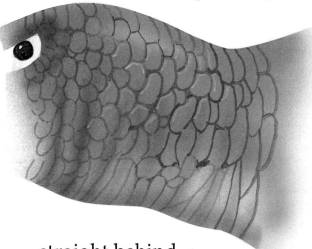

Clawed hands

At the end of **Megalosaurus**'s very short forelimbs were three clawed fingers. These must have been useful for clutching prey.

Short neck

As you can see at the right, **Megalosaurus** had a short, thick, flexible neck.

straight behind as it lumbered along. These pointers should help you identify a **Megalosaurus** in a museum collection.

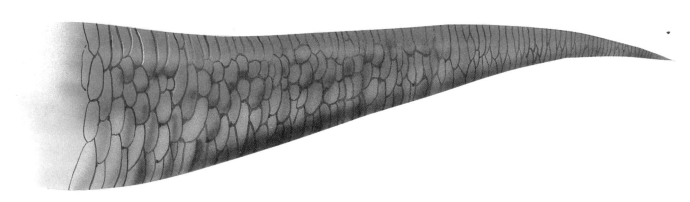

The Megalosaurid gang

Megalosaurus (1) had several close relatives, known by the group name of **Megalosaurids**.

These giant meat-eaters all lived in Jurassic or Cretaceous times.

You can see some of them on these two pages.

Jurassic **Eustreptospondylus** (YOO-STREP-TOE-SPON-DEE-LUSS) **(2)** lived in what are now England and France. About 23 feet (7 m) long, it had a large head and sharp teeth.

Gasosaurus (GAS-O-SAW-RUS) **(3)** was named in honor of the natural gas industry for its help in discovering this dinosaur a few years ago in China. Gasosaurus lived in Jurassic times and was a 13-foot (4-m)-long, 8-foot (2.5-m)-tall carnivore with curved fangs and clawed hands.

Although small when compared to many of its relatives, **Gasosaurus** would still have towered above you. It would have been a feared predator, boldly attacking for food.

Remains of **Altispinax** (AL-TEE-SPINE-AX) **(4)** — whose name means "tall spines" — have been found in Germany and southeastern England. It, too, was a dreadful carnivore and one of the larger **Megalosaurids**. But the tall spines on its back that formed a sort of sail made this Cretaceous dinosaur look a little different from the rest of the **Megalosaurid** gang.

When dinosaurs like these were around, it was time for smaller creatures to make a quick exit!

GLOSSARY

carnivores — meat-eating animals.

extinction — the dying out of all members of a plant or animal species.

fangs — long, pointed teeth used by animals to hold their victims or inject poison.

fossils — traces or remains of plants and animals found in rock.

herbivores — plant-eating animals.

predators — animals that capture and kill other animals for food.

prey — animals captured and killed for food by other animals.

quarry — a place where stone or marble is excavated, or dug up, from the ground.

remains — a skeleton, bones, or a dead body.

reptiles — cold-blooded animals that have hornlike or scale-covered skin.

spikes — pointed objects used to pierce or cut.

trek — a difficult, slow-moving journey or expedition.

INDEX

24